ADVICE FOR LIFE: WORDS OF WISDOM, HOPE & INSPIRATION

Dr. Debra Patricia Shipp

D1715583

ADVICE FOR LIFE: WORDS OF WISDOM, HOPE & INSPIRATION

Dr. Debra Patricia Shipp

478 284 6971

A Lily Inc. book published by Lily Inc., a publishing and printing company.   www.Lilyinc.net   240 765 8705
Lilyinc@Lilyinc.net   Lilyinc@ymail.com

ISBN: 9798634359137

First Edition April 5, 2020

Written by Dr. Debra Patricia Shipp and
 Edited by Clarence Thomas Jr.

Printed in the United States of America, Macon GA, and South Carolina.

******For information regarding special discounts on bulk purchases, contact Dr. Debra Patricia Shipp
@debrashipp1@gmail.com 478 284 6971*****

This book is dedicated to God, my family and Sister Ellen Miller. All of whom have had a great, favorable impact on my life.

It is also in memory of my parents S.B. and JoAnn McGhee, who provided me with a good foundation and are a source of strength even beyond the grave

~Dr. Debra McGhee Shipp

Now is the time for all of us to be watchful, to pray and be as Christ like as possible to ensure that we stay in God's grace; and how we heal the world
~ Sister Ellen Miller

Contents

FOREWORD

What began in early December 2018 culminates in the form of this book by Dr. Debra McGhee Shipp. *Advice for Life: Words of Wisdom, Hope and Inspiration*, started as her desire to share portions of her life experiences coupled with recommendations on righteous living inspired by the word of God and her friend and spiritual teacher Sister Ellen Miller.

As the producer of this product our company had the privilege of conducting and transcribing hours of interviews of Dr. Shipp; co-editing the book; assisting with the publishing process and publicizing this vision of its creator.

While these are the technical aspects of the book's formulation, it was the human interaction with Dr. Shipp, Sister Ellen and the publisher Glow of Light LLC that made the journey special. Each of us poured ourselves into making this divinely inspired read a tangible resource of help to humanity.

This book is an extension of who Dr. Shipp is— a concerned, caring member of the human family that shares her passion and gifts with her family and community through her evangelism, businesses and direct outreach. As a result, you're in for a real treat. So, fasten your seatbelts, hold on to something and prepare to be moved and amazed by *Advice for Life: Words of Wisdom, Hope and Inspiration*!

Clarence Thomas, Jr.

CEO/Communications Director Visionary Communications...*THE Communications Source in the Info Age* Macon, Georgia   478-952-8218

thomas1963@cox.net thomasjr63@gmail.com
Facebook/Visionary Communications Instagram/Visionary 2003

Introduction

Giving all glory to God who makes all things possible. Like this book for instance. It was born out of the longtime support and inspiration, and friendship of my spiritual mother Ellen Miller, whose been there for me the last 26 years before and since losing my birth mother JoAnn McGhee in 2013. Sister Miller is truly a woman of God. She is a prophet, woman of wisdom and my best friend. She has always given me great advice in numerous situations concerning what's right and what's wrong. She has kept me on the right path by imparting the word of God in my life and encouraging me always to do what is right in the eyes of the Lord. Sister Ellen has helped me become the woman of God that I am today. She has even prophesized things that have happened to me countless times. And for as long as I've known Sister Ellen, she has remained faithful and consistent in her faith and love for God. She is still an energetic 89-year-old woman of God and Pastor of Faith Walk in Action Ministry in Macon, GA. God put me in her spirit nearly three decades ago as we met at a local church. She has helped me with biblical principles throughout most of my entire life. This book is dedicated to her. It's comprised of simple quotes, words of wisdom and inspiration.

My goal within these pages is to help people to know that whatever you are going through, you can overcome it just by applying some of these words of wisdom, principals, and quotes to your lives. This book serves not only as a testament to how valuable Sister Ellen has been to me, but as a reminder to us of how great God is by blessing her with the gift of wisdom that she has shared with me through simple valuable truths. I want it to also serve as a guiding light in life regarding how we should walk daily as it transcends borders and becomes a source of strength and as a resource concerning how we should be living.

Thanks for purchasing it. I pray that it will prove to be a worthwhile return on your investment. And remember…you can do all things through Christ that strengthens you. (Philippians 4:13) May this offering help you to both believe and achieve your dreams. Blessing!
~ *Dr. Debra McGhee Shipp*

Just Do What's Right!

James 4:17
So, whoever knows the right thing to do and fails to do it, for him it is sin.

Proverbs 14:34
Righteousness exalts a nation, but sin condemns any people:

Sister Ellen always said, "Debra Just Do What's Right". It doesn't matter what everybody is doing, you do what's right. Just do what is right according to the word of God. I guarantee you will be blessed. As Christians it is incumbent upon us to do what's right anyway. She reminded me that as I practice doing what's right, to "Watch God in the Process!" She said the eyes of the Lord are in every place beholding the good and the evil. She told me that he sees everything that we do and hears all that we say. Remember he is watching. You cannot hide from him. There have been many instances that I wanted to tear people apart. I wanted revenge!!! I was hurting and had been hurt tremendously by others. There were times when I really wanted to fight back physically. But I couldn't. I found out and learned that doing what's right anyway pays off tremendously. If I could just hold my peace and let the Lord fight my battles, then I knew victory would be mine. I am here to let you know that God will fight your battles and come to your rescue every time. That is...... if you let him.

Proverbs 21:2 says, "You see A man's ways seem right in his own eyes, but the Lord weighs the heart". We cannot handle our own situations in our own way. No, that won't work. We must do them God's way. We must deny the flesh. We cannot do what we want to do when we want to do it. Often the devil will trick us into handling our own situations, but we must be aware! We must honor the word of God. Often our flesh begs for us to get even, but we must not do that. Two wrongs do not make any situation right. For the Scripture Romans 12:19 says "Vengeance is mine sayeth the Lord: I will repay thee".

I'm reminded of a time and circumstance that happened to me in the past where I had to apply doing what's right to my very own life. For instance, when my parents died. It was a terrible time for me. It was horrific. My father S.B. McGhee passed on January 15, 2013 and my mom died four and a half months later. In the mist of my sorrow, I was attacked by my entire family, physically, spiritually, and emotionally. I didn't have time to grieve. I was trying to do what my parents requested and taught us all those years. I was trying to explain the climactic truth to everyone about the aggression that I faced from my family, but nobody would believe me. It was the strangest thing…. nobody believed me!

I was stunned that people wanted to hurt me and enjoyed seeing me hurt. What was so sad was that people rejoiced at my hurt. I was very tempted to fight back, but Sister Ellen advised me again to do what was right even under such trying circumstances. You see I had lost my parents and I was under constant attacks from family. Sister Ellen reminded me that you are the one that says that you are saved and so you cannot act the way the world acts.

You are to be the example. In my mind…. I didn't want to be the example, but I needed God for strength. Here again I had to deny the flesh. So, I prayed with a friend and I was able to do what was right. So, I remained humbled and nice to relatives, and friends that were visiting during the family visitations in preparation of funeralizing my parents.

I lost two parents, but God gave me the strength to rise

above the turmoil. I felt like I had been stabbed in my heart by everything that had happened to me. I couldn't understand it at all. Why would anyone want to hurt me? What did I do Lord to deserve this? It took some time to get over it all and be healed as to what had happened but years later God changed things. It was all because I had taken Sister Ellen's advice, received guidance from the Holy Spirit and did what was right anyway. Doing right can be very difficult at times but I can honestly say it pays off. God fought my battles for me and now I feel so free.

After all that hurt and pain of losing my mom and dad, I then experience another situation in which I had to do what was right. This instance happened in the church. Yes! The hospital for Christians. I faced Church Hurt! I was Rejected by the Church. I faced much abuse, jealousy, envy and rejection in the church. I was just being who God called me to be. I was applying my anointing and gifts while at church and guess what. I was wronged again. Now you have not faced any hurt until you have experience Church hurt. I pray that if you are facing this that you really lean and depend on God.

My problem was that I loved everybody just too hard. I would always give my best, but it was prophesied to me that I would be "Often Misunderstood" by people of this world. Especially Church People. I was abused by insecure leaders and insecure leadership. I could not understand this because I had not been raised in the church to act this way. I simply had not been exposed to this type of behavior. Not only that, but I felt as though the church was the hospital and found out that it was a place that I had experienced my greatest pain. A lot of things happened to me but being raised in a home by two great parents and spoiled by my father helped. Nevertheless, I began to meet people who were going to show me that I wasn't going to get my way in the church. Their intention was to show me that I'm the Boss and you will do as I say. I wondered what was going on in the church. Why Lord? I didn't know I was being punished or even being led by hurt people. It is then that I learned a lesson that hurt people hurt others. "God I still got to do what's right? Are you kidding me? "I pondered. I'm trying to do what's right and I am being punished and attacked by a past that stemmed partially from me being my dad's daughter coupled with insecurity on their behalf.

However, I continued to be nice, show respect, praise God, pay my tithe and offering and smile. God kept me! I did what was right in the eyes of the Lord and guess what.... years later some of those church members came to me and said how sorry they were they had treated me that way and how much they wanted me to return. Doing the right thing does pay off. When we do what's right, God will exalt us. It feels good to do the right thing. It is his expectation.

What happens is we often try to help God out. We get in our own way. We must reference God's will when deciding what to do. Operating in wisdom is the key. When we do the right thing, it's rewarding. I believe it makes God smile because we're doing what he says to do. It creates peace in us and in our fellow man. It builds character. It's a blessing to other people. Doing the right thing makes us feel free. There's a freedom in it that you can't put a price tag on.

People can see your strength in doing the right thing. Because observers know you've been abused, hurt, dejected and rejected. But in the process, they see a person doing the right thing despite their challenges and it compels the observer to embrace this position as well. Sometimes it's good to let them see you sweat! If you sweat; I guarantee you will come out on top. Just do what's right.

Just Forgive Them

Matthew 6:14-15
For if you forgive other people when they sin against you your heavenly father will also forgive you. But if you do not forgive others their sins, your father will not forgive your sins

It's best to forgive. God forgave us for all our sins, so we should forgive others when they offend us. No matter what someone has done to us, we must forgive. Because forgiveness is not for the other person, it's for us. Meaning that it removes a weight off us. When you forgive others sincerely if takes away a load on us. And we should ask the Holy Spirit to intercede and help us to forgive since the spirit is willing, but the flesh is weak. We're never going to forget what others have done to us, but with God's help we can forgive. Forgiveness creates a wonderful feeling within. It allows us to say hello, be cordial, pray for them and act in accordance with what God wants us to be. God forgave us repeatedly.

Not forgiving is like a cancer. It eats away at us because we're holding onto something that's not good. The tendency is to hold grudges. That makes us bitter. But when we release what others have done to offend us, then we become stress free and reap physical benefits as well. And forgiving is personal and has value. This simple principle helps a lot of people because it keeps us from stopping ourselves for moving forward. It allows us to not get in our own way. Not forgiving is like a roadblock. You can't go through, over, under or around it and can't get to your destination.

Forgiveness allows us to think and act clearer. The adage "If you change the way you look at things, the way you look at things will change" then makes more sense. Forgiving has allowed me to be the woman that I am today. It has opened doors for me. It's something that we must do. When you come to that place you feel so free. If we want God to forgive us, then we must be willing to forgive. When we do, The Creator will throw our shortcomings in the sea of forgetfulness, remember it no more and bless us over and over.

My spiritual mother Sister Ellen used to remind me when it was obvious that I was holding on to grudges after being betrayed. She would say, "You haven't forgiven. You must forgive in order to receive." I thought I had, but she would persist and insist that I do. I have forgiven people that hurt me. And it has confused those that I did. When we forgive, it lets us ease on down the road. Fight every battle on your knees. I guarantee that you will win every time. Just simply forgive them.

Love Everybody

1 John 4 and 7-8
Dear friends, let us love one another, for love comes from God. Everyone who loves has been born of God and knows God. Whoever does not love does not know God, because God is love ...

1 Corinthians: 13:4-8
Love is patient, love is kind, it does not envy. It does not boast, it is not proud, it does not dishonor others. It is not self-seeking; it is not easily angered. It keeps no record of wrongs. Love does not delight in evil but rejoices with the truth. It always protects, always trust, always hopes, always preserves. Love never fails.

It's tough to love someone that has wronged you. That includes the church, family and friends. But love covers a multitude of sins. Of all the gifts the greatest one is love. Love is a verb and not a noun. You can tell someone all day long that you do, but if your action says otherwise, then maybe you don't. Love is patient. Love is kind. Love is a beautiful thing. In most of my situations I have loved and didn't get it in return. Nevertheless, I chose to love despite this. We should have love inside of us, come out and show others how to love.

There's power in loving. It creates a feeling of peace and cultivates a spirit of happiness that is infectious. Loving sets off endorphins that produce positive responses within us emotionally and physically. You can't put a price on love. The late great actress, renowned poet and writer **Maya Angelou** said, "love recognizes no barriers. It jumps hurdles, leaps fences, penetrates walls to arrive at its destination full of hope." Love is what love does. If you have love inside of you, then you will show it. My mother use to say, "Girl a mouth will say anything. People will tell you anything." But when true love transpires between people it will serve all involved. It opens us up to each other. It opens our heart to God. Because he said, "if you love me, you keep my commandments." Anything else other than what he says or wants, is the devil. God is love. If you don't have the love of God in your heart, then you are not his. How can you love God whom you've never seen, and hate your neighbor whom you see all the time? We must have love.

There's no way around it.

Do Something Different

Isaiah 43:19
See, I am doing a new thing! Now it springs up, do you not perceive it? I am making a way in the wilderness and streams in the wasteland

Ezekiel 36:26
And I will give you a new heart and a new spirit I will put within you.

Jeremiah 29:11
For I know the plans I have for you, declares the Lord, plans for welfare and not for evil to give you future and hope.

Trying other things is important, because so many of the old

things we're doing are not working. The Bible says, "Behold I

make all things new." Some things are unforgettable, like

history. But God says he's doing a new thing. When we are in

touch with God, he will give us something new and different to

do. For instance, instead of having church inside, weather

permitting go outside and have it on the church lawn or at a

community center. My *Chat and* Chew *Ministry* is an example

of going outside of the box. We chat and chew about almost

anything. We take it to the water! It allows us to casually converse and commune over food about God and his desire for us. Allow him to show you his purpose. It might be making cupcakes with words of love or wisdom on them. It might be putting those words on school pencils to keep our children moving in a positive direction in the classroom. The great inventor and philosopher **George Washington Carver** – made famous for his discovery of a multitude of usages for the peanut – said, "When you can do the common things in life in an uncommon way, you will command the attention of the world". I will add to that, God's attention as well.

When we do something different, I believe that God really smiles on us, because we're offering something new and different for people to choose from. God will give you new and fresh ideas.

Everybody has purpose. Let's wash people's feet. Let's pamper the elderly. Let's write scriptures in the sand. Let's give people free massages. When we think of something, we must ask God to help us overcome our fear of doing something. We must be like the Nike phrase, "Just Do It!". A lot of times we can't do things

on our own. That's when fasting and praying pays off. Once we do,

we become open to God speaking to us and doing what he instructs

us to do

There are a lot of things that can be done by thinking and acting

out of the box. Things can be done by stepping out on faith and being

receptive to change. You got to be able to see it. Because if you can

see it, you can achieve it. Fly like an eagle and don't have the

buzzard mentality.

Think of Others Before Yourself

Philippians 2:3
*Do nothing out of selfish ambition or vain conceit, but in humility
consider others better than yourselves. Each of you should look not
only to your own interests, but also to the interest of others. But
made himself nothing, taking the very nature of a servant, being
made in human likeness*

We really love ourselves. We want the best for ourselves. God

wants us to show that same love for others that we show ourselves.

It's good to love your fellow man. It's good to be neighborly. The

person sitting next to you in church. The person living next door to

us in our neighborhood. You do need to be kind to them. Think to yourself, "I wouldn't do harm to myself. I wouldn't do anything to hurt myself." So, we should have this same attitude about others that we have for ourselves.

To do this, we must have the Holy Spirit of God in us. Keep in mind that we should have the attitude that, "I want for this person what I want for myself. I want to treat this person the way I want to be treated." If this is difficult, then we should get good teaching and guidance. Scripture is a good reference. Bear in mind that in order to love others we must love ourselves first.

A Biblical figure that comes to mind is Joseph. He still looked out for his family and other people when he became governor, despite being hated by many before becoming governor. Mary and Martha washed the feet of Jesus. An act of putting him before their pride. Former First Lady **Michelle Obama** suggests that, "success isn't about how much money you make. It's about the difference you make in people's lives." The late legendary heavyweight boxing champion and humanitarian known as The Greatest, **Muhammad Ali** called "service to others the rent we pay for our room on Earth."

Thinking of others in our action catches on. By becoming caretakers of each other, we become a real genuine collective. We become neighborhood watchmen. It makes it easier to get each other's back. We must give something in order to get something. If you want a good neighbor, you can do a simple act of kindness. Work with each other to make sure your yards look good. Share information or goods with each other. Watch their home when they're away.

When we give out of our hearts, our neighbors tend to give back in turn. Although we don't give to receive, it's a natural response by those we do nice things for.

Mother Ellen always said, "Always be cordial. Be kind. You don't have to kiss their backside but be kind." She said to speak to people, respond to them when they reach out. Be watchful and pray. She really believes in giving to others what you want for yourself.

Everyone Has Gifts: Use Them

1 Corinthians 12
There are different kinds of gifts, but the same spirit. There are different kinds of service, but the same Lord… All these are the work of one and the same spirit and he gives them to each one, just as he determines

Romans 12:6-8

We have different gifts, according to the grace given to each of us. If your gift is prophesying, then prophesy in accordance with your faith; if it is serving, then serve; if it is teaching, then teach; if it is to encourage, then give encouragement; if is giving, then give generously; if it is to lead, do it diligently; if it is to show mercy, do it cheerfully.

We should pursue our gifts because each of us are fearfully and wonderfully made. Everybody is different. We are like snowflakes. Snowflakes are all comprised of the same thing for the same purpose, but no two are the same. Each one is unique. Every person is different. No two people are the same. Everybody has gifts and purpose. But what we must do is seek the Lord. You have to go before him and ask God, "What is my gift? What should I be doing?"

People that are vocal, demanding and argumentative for example might want to work in the church parking lot directing car traffic. No harm intended, but you must get into a position with God for him to show you your gift. Because we can be doing a lot of different things, but is it what God wants us to be doing? There was a time when I was involved in a lot of things, because it's what I wanted to do. But God showed me over time that that some of those things were not in accordance with what he wanted me to be doing. I had to learn that it wasn't about what I wanted, but what he wanted. I believe in fasting and praying. God will show us the way when we sacrifice and ask him to reveal what's best for us.

My god brother Milton's mother wanted him to be a doctor and he went to school to be a chiropractor, but he didn't like what he was doing as a professional. He eventually decided to decorate houses instead and is doing exceptionally well as an Interior Designer. His mother didn't see the logic in his decision at the time and questioned his judgement. Today however his business Milton Miller's Interiors is excelling, and in addition, making a lot of money and gaining notoriety on social media platforms. He also has made national television appearances and is working in Atlanta and abroad. Milton is a master Interior Designer. He is as content as can be and exceptionally happy doing what he really wanted to do and what likely God ordained him to do. When you find your purpose, living is relaxing, rewarding and easy because you've found your reason for existing.

Gifts come in various forms. There's the gift of prophecy. The gift of gab. The gift of servitude. The gift of ministry. There's the gift of leadership. And many more. Sometimes however people try to force a gift on themselves. Our gifts should come naturally. My *Chat and Chew* Ministry is an example and definitely a gift from God. I love to talk and have a bite to eat as I do it. It's very involved, consuming and demanding. And can sometimes wear me out. However, I love it because it's so rewarding and an extension of who I am and what I'm about. As a result, doing this ministry comes easy in the end.

We should always thank God for our gifts. He is to get all the glory for what he has given us to give the world. The scriptures say in Psalms 39: 12, "If I had ten thousand tongues, it wouldn't be enough to praise God." We can thank him by simply giving him our time. It might be in the car while driving. Or it might be while waiting to meet with someone. We owe God time and praise. We owe him everything. We must give him our time and talent. We owe each other as humans too. When we don't share our gifts, we deny humanity a chance to benefit from what God has blessed us to provide through them. That plate you fixed for a hungry person, that tissue you handed somebody when they were distraught or that prayer you prayed for them when they were sick can make all the difference in the world.

Sadly, some people see your gifts, but don't want them to exist. Envy, jealously, competition and insecurity can cause some people to try to impede your gift. Prayer is a strong point of mine. I prayed on several occasions at alters resulting in some people passing out even. They later shared the improvements in their lives directly or indirectly and thanked me for praying for them. But I was always quick to remind them that it was God working through me, not Debra Shipp that made the difference. Some people couldn't believe that I produced this kind of result and questioned my ability and the authenticity of those that benefitted. Nonetheless, I persevered, endured and remained prayerful. In addition, I remained patient and respectful to my leaders. I advise you to do the same. It's necessary if you are committed to being a blessing to the world

and making a difference in the lives of those ready to benefit from your gifts.

Gossiping ...and Why We Shouldn't

Proverbs 16:28
A perverse person stirs up conflict and a gossip separate close friends

Proverbs 11:13
A gossip betrays a confidence, but a trustworthy person keeps a secret.

To me gossiping is talking to much about other's business that we may not know fully about if anything to multiple people. It tends to go on and on. Gossip is like lying because it's spreading news that may or may not be true about others. Gossiping is bad because it facilitates us meddling in other's affairs that don't concern us. There's a saying that "Sticks and stones may break my bones, but names will never hurt me." But words hurt. Others meddling in our affairs without knowledge hurts. God hates a lying tongue. Proverbs tells us to be careful about how we speak and to get wisdom. Gossiping is a form of evil. Sometimes people gossip because they want to take the spotlight off themselves and cast it onto others. People that gossip lack a certain amount of intelligence and integrity. The Bible says there's life and death in the tongue.

The human in us tends to love gossip. But we must allow our

better self to prevail and stay away from partaking of it. If we are the gossiper, then we need to ask God to bridle our tongue. We must ask him to help us with our mouth. Treating it like a fast is a good exercise. We all have the potential to talk too much. Through trial and error, I myself had to learn to curb my talking. Doing this requires discipline and commitment.

We forget that while others are the unfortunate recipient of gossip, the gossiper forgets that they are hurt as well. I once heard about a woman that was publicly expressing her business concerning her caretaking of her husband and the benefits associated with her taking care of him. She expressed that he didn't want to come to the affair that we were at, but that she was getting paid to bring him anyway. However, those present were embarrassed for him because he lacked the ability to tell her to stop spreading his and her business randomly. They felt that it was information they didn't need to hear. Proverbs also says, "whosoever goes about babbling secrets should be avoided." Ephesians recommends to "Let no corrupt talk to come out of your mouth."

Instead of spreading gossip, use your mouth to build the kingdom of God. Let others know how good God is instead. But you must pray to him and let him show you when, where and how you should speak. Sing a song instead. Say a speech full of good. Be someone's spokesperson. Be a host or hostess instead. Mother Miller once suggested to someone that she was talking too much, and that she should spend more time listening instead. That advice is sound and advice that I adhere to. I suggest this for you as well.

God Is the Sufficient Source in Battle

2nd Chronicles 20:15
He said "Listen, King Jehoshaphat and all who live in Judah and Jerusalem! This is what the Lord says to you: "Do not be afraid or discouraged because of this vast army. For the battle is not yours, but Gods!

Why should we fight battles that are already won? Because scripture says that "vengeance is mine thus saith the Lord." It also says the battle is God's not ours. However, there are times when we must stand up for ourselves and stand up for righteousness. But don't do an eye for an eye. First, in a potential conflict we should ask God what we must do. Next before proceeding we should fight in the spiritual realm by fasting and praying and then handing it over to God. Try to get someone to pray with you. Mother Ellen said you can get more done by praying about a situation than talking about it all the time. Talking about something repeatedly equals rehearsal. And it can get into our spirits. Talking about it repeatedly can make you upset and angry all over again. The early 20th century scholar, activist and cofounder of the National Association for the Advancement of Colored People (NAACP) W.E.B. **Dubois** suggested that, "there is in this world no such force as the force of a person determined to rise. The human soul cannot be permanently chained."

God wants us to not be afraid. He has not given us the spirit of fear but of sound mind. With his help we can do anything. We have power. He gave us power to overcome different things. He promised to protect us. He said he would never leave or forsake us. We don't have to be afraid. We must stand our ground when necessary because nothing should separate us from him and what's right. Sometimes you will be alone. This is especially true in ministry. Stand your ground. Because right is going to prevail over wrong always.

The enemy will then see that the righteous shall not be moved. The enemy will know that you cannot be used or abused. And your respect will remain intact When you put on th whole armor of God, you will stand and win. The reward of righteously resting are awesome.

Suffering: Don't Look Like What You've Been Through

Colossians 3:12
You are the people of God; he loved you and chose you for his own, so then, you must clothe yourselves with compassion, kindness, humility, gentleness and patience

Psalm 46:10
Be still and know that I am God

Romans 5:3-4
Not only so, but we also glory in our sufferings, because we know that suffering produces perseverance, *character and hope*

Suffering is not in vain. We suffer so that God can get the glory out of our lives. It's painful. It hurts. It feels bad. It's tough. It can put you in a place that you've never been in your life where you feel like nothing. James 1 says, "consider it joy when you face trials of many kinds, for it is a testament of your faith." Another scripture says weeping endures but a night, but joy comes in the morning.

God wants to see if we are going to be mature and complete about praising him and glorying him even in suffering. Grammy nominated gospel music sensation **Jekalyn Carr** talks about suffering in one of her hit songs where she sang about being bruised and beaten. But in it she reminds us eventually that God is preparing us for something greater. So, suffering is made to make us stronger. The late 19th century abolitionist, scholar, orator and former slave **Frederick Douglass** said simply, "if there is no struggle, there is no progress.

Power concedes nothing without a demand. It never did and it never will."

Sometimes we wonder where God is when we are suffering. We think that he has forgotten or left us. He's carrying us during this time. He's right there. He allows suffering to take place in our lives intentionally because we would continue to do the same old thing. Think about Jesus. He suffered much for us. But by his stripes we are healed.

Consider what takes place when we suffer. Because suffering is very uncomfortable, we don't want to repeat getting whipped. We know that sin is a trigger for suffering. Like when we were children. Those whippings we earned in most cases hurt. They were unforgiving because the old people didn't play when they finally had to pull out a belt or pick a switch off the tree. So, like the childhood experiences, the pain associated with suffering for sinning keeps us in check. Jesus suffered significantly for us. He was beaten all night long, crowned with thorns, made to carry a cross until he couldn't and later nailed to it until he died a slow, tortuous death. He took on our sins for us.

As absurd as it sounds, we must suffer properly to reap the dividends in the end. We still must be grateful. We still must glorify God. We still must treat others with dignity and respect. We still must be kind. How do we do this? We must deny ourselves. There are numerous forms of suffering. We suffer in our finances. We suffer at the hands of family and friends. We suffer because of a lack of knowledge. However, we must go through in order to get to.

And it's not just going through, but how we go through it. A lot of times we put on a good face as though we aren't hurting when we are going through something. We camouflage our pain with smiles and assurances that we are OK. We wear a mask as well because we fear being perceived as deserving of whatever trial we are going through. "She's getting what she earned," say some. "What in the world did he do?" observers ask each other. Some people love for others to go through something. They rejoice in the suffering of others. They like it.

But we still must maintain our integrity, humor, dignity and positivity when we are suffering. We react differently to suffering. Some people worry. Some stop seeing the humor in things. Sometimes we get angry at others, including God. But we must remain steadfast and still give glory to him. Because the scripture says that in everything give glory to God. In all things give thanks. We still must do this. When we suffer and we thank God for his wisdom anyway, we win. While we're suffering, we still must give him thanks and praise. Thank him for the pain. Thank him for the other side of the suffering. We must praise God in season and out of season. No matter what the current situation is we are still obligated to praise him.

When the praises go up the blessings come down. Suffering should compel us to get down on our knees and call on God like never before. Seeking relief is a good reason to not tarry.

Sometimes suffering comes because we haven't given The Most High enough of our time and attention. In turn he will allow things to happen so we can get back to him. God might say sometimes, "Let me let that washing machine go down." or "Let me let your water bill be higher this billing cycle." These are ways that God gets our attention and guides us back to giving him the time and attention he desires and deserves. But thankfully God says, "Come unto me all ye that labor, and I will give you rest." He is always there waiting to provide relief.

It seems that if he is the cause of our suffering, then he wouldn't be there to relieve us. However, he is merciful and gracious. He anxiously awaits us.

Sometimes our suffering is for others. In this case, what we endure is for our detractors. During the early development of this book, my spiritual mother Ellen was suffering over several nights in excruciating pain. When I asked her how bad her pain was on a scale of 1-10, she said it was a 20. That's because she had a sciatica nerve in her back. It's been said having one is very uncomfortable. But even in pain she called out, "God thank you! I know you're speaking to me. I know I'm suffering for someone else. I receive it! I know this is something I'm going through for someone else." She was talking to herself. And it wasn't the first time she had been through this. She was suffering for other people. Sometimes it's necessary. Jesus suffered for us.

So, what is the value in suffering? Even though it's hard and hurts, I believe that it builds strength and character. It makes you stronger and helps you to see things for what they are. Sometimes it can beat you down so low until you feel like dirt on the ground, but when you come up you can see a whole lot better. You can see the whole picture. Because you've been beat down it's a denial of the flesh. This experience causes us to see things in another light. Without rain in our lives, we can't appreciate sunshine.

We are going to suffer. But trouble don't last always. Some people always have a sad story. God doesn't do anything for them ever according them. They're always negative. These are people that won't count it all joy. These are the ones that don't understand why the righteous must suffer as well. These are the ones that don't believe that life isn't always easy.

God didn't say that life was going to be easy. He didn't say we weren't going to have purges. Sometimes what we go through can be from our actions in our past.

Let's possess a Job spirit. When going through his trial and tribulations he stated, "The Lord gave and the Lord has taken away, blessed be the name of the Lord." During our suffering we still must stay at it. Stay the course. Keep God first. This is not the time to pull away from God. This is the time to get rooted in him the most. Be guarded and stay focused. If we're not this could turn in a period of us developing a noncaring attitude. Don't do this. This is the time to run to God. Because we might seek to find comfort in things not good for us. Remember, no test, no testimony. If we don't pass the test the first time around, we will have to go through again.

That's why some people keep going around and around.

They haven't passed the test. They haven't learned to love the people that hurt them. They're still mad at them. When you suffer you must know how to go through it. You must continue to praise God. Stay before the Lord. Fast and pray. And surround yourself with a good group of people that can support you. Because everybody needs someone to help them when they are going through something. We are not Superman. You need someone to speak hope to you. That's why I value my spiritual mother so because she always had something encouraging to say to me when I was weak or down about what I was going through. In addition, there is a reason for our suffering. But suffering properly makes for good testimonials.

I once had to attend dinner with a person that I didn't like that much. And to add injury to insult, the person tended to brag the whole time I was around them. Especially about material things. But because I had committed to breaking bread with that person, I stayed the course despite my reservation about doing dinner with that individual. I asked God, "How am I going to get through this in a way that is pleasing to you? Should I proceed or not?" I did and was led by the Holy Spirit to do it the way he guided me to do it. Because I denied myself, I was able to speak a word into that person and our dinner turned out to be a beautiful undertaking. I passed that test because I was willing to persevere and work through the situation.

We've all heard the phrase, "I don't look like what I've been through." This is a true statement if you can camouflage your hurt, shame and pain. But it shouldn't be artificially masked. It should be in our ability to turn pain into joy. Take your suffering and flip it. My mantra regarding this is… "I'm not my own. I belong to Christ. I was bought with a price. I truly belong to him." Whatever happens is ordained by God. Case in point, I know a lady that had a wreck. She later had another wreck and fall. She often talked about retiring. But her son intervened after her car wreck and conveyed to her that he no longer wanted her driving following the wreck. Because she wasn't at fault, she was able to collect sustainable compensation and retire on disability immediately. So, what the devil meant for bad, became something good for her. When this happens, we need to count it all joy. You can take something bad and turn it into something good. If you change how you look at things, the way you look at things will change.

Hearing and Obeying God

John 10:27
My sheep hear my voice, and I know them, and they follow me.

Proverbs 3:5
In with all thy getting, get understanding

We must hear God. We must be hearers and doers of his word. Sometimes we get to busy to hear him because we're so busy doing other things. We must get into a position to hear him. When we go all the time, we're not able to hear from God. Say no sometime. Put down your electronic devices. Run that errand later. At one point I was doing a whole lot, but it was impeding my ability to hear from God. But he ran interference on that so that I could hear from him. A lot of time we can be all over the place. And we shouldn't take on too much. Pastors are especially vulnerable. They tend to take on so much sometimes that they can hardly endure. Their care for those they serve can become overwhelming. In some cases, however, pastors let ego and insecurity cause them to take on too much because they want to be the center of attention. This is wrong. Because we must do what we do for God's glory and for his people. When we don't hear his call, he will get our attention. God will sit us down! It's to get our attention. We must listen to God. We must come clean.

When we ignore God and don't submit then things will continue to happen until we hear him. God is saying "I've given you the plan, but you want to do it your way." But God says, "if you love me you will obey my commandments." And when we hear God, we will want to be a clean vessel for him. Being clean allows us to be better deliverers of his word and better examples to those looking on. It requires faith as well. Faith equals trust in God and his deliverance. Hebrews 11:6 says, "without faith it is impossible to please him for whoever would draw near to God must believe that he exits and that he rewards those that seek him." Hearing and obeying God allows us to be in his perfect will. This allows us to receive his benefits and blessings and all things he has promised us. This is when overflow and walking in the right relationship with him occurs. God says, "I will keep those in perfect peace that listen to me". We need to listen to God productively. Each time we read scripture for instance he is speaking to us. So, when we hear him, he will guide us in all truths. This is when the Holy Spirit gives us insight and discernment increases. I once prayed for a family that had lost a son. When hugging the wife, I really felt her pain and suffering but when hugging his mother, I felt nothing. Later I found out that his mother and sisters were challenged in a way that had created an inability to feel pain in the manner his wife did. Nevertheless, God urged me to reach out to them despite their inability to reciprocate my outreach.

Hearing and obeying God in this case gave me a sense of peace because I done what he guided me to do anyway. When we hear him, it allows us to better minister to others. Hearing God will save us a lot of heartache and pain. It changes our lives. The Holy Spirit will be able to better guide us. As my momma said, "You might not hear from me but you're going to hear from somebody." The old folks said that "A hard head makes for a soft behind." We must be able to let God speak to us and tell us what and when to do his will.

Possess a Discerning Spirit

1 John: 4:1
Beloved do not believe every spirit, but test the spirits to see whether they are from God, for many false prophets have gone out into the world

The spirit of discernment is awesome. It will tell you what to say, when and how to say something. It will keep you out of a lot of trouble. It will allow you to be kind anyway under trying circumstances. It will allow you to choose wisely. It will afford you the ability to see into things. And not cuss someone out that deserves it! **Harriet Tubman**, who led countless slaves to freedom as a conductor on the Underground Railroad reminded us that, "every great dream begins with a dreamer. Always remember, you have within you the strength, the patience, and the passion to reach for the stars to change the world." You must act in wisdom and not the flesh. There is a lady that I'm affiliated with that was watching and learning from me. So, I had to be careful how I carried myself and how I spoke to her. She was not a good listener and had problems following my instructions. But rather than getting frustrated with her and communicating to her in a manner that reflected my frustration, I chose to correct her with a kind, sensitive spirit that gave her the chance to improve and get better at assisting me.

Take pause and don't be so quick to react when dealing with

people. Discern the situation, adjust and then proceed. Doing things in this manner will facilitate a better outcome.

Leadership: What It Looks Like & How It Should Operate

Matthew 7:12
So, in everything, do   unto others what you would have them do to you, for this sums up the Law and prophets
Philippians 4:13
I can do all this through him who gives me strength

John Quincy Adams, the son of John Adams - one of the founding fathers of our country, said, "if your actions inspire others to dream more, learn more, do more and become more, you are a leader." Good leadership is seamless and should look like the personal life of the leader. If a leader's personal house in is order, then that leader should be able to run the church, business or organization in an orderly, controlled fashion. Those that are close to us and how they react and act around us as others observe is telling. If those you're in charge of remain supportive and respectful, then you are likely a good leader unless those you're leading can't discern very well. But is there's a shift in how they treat you or if they never get on board, then a self-check is in order. Those under that kind of leader should then proceed with praying for them. Lending advice is not viable since bad leaders tend to not listen to anyone except themselves. They lack transparency and have trouble being authentic. In addition, they're close minded, inconsistent and harbor huge egos. This is not good.

In environments like work for instance, it can be very counterproductive because it can cause workplace leaders to ride people unnecessarily, be controlling, unfair and unreasonable. To rectify this the leader must own their shortcomings and get to work on changing and leading by example. Sometimes our life is the only Bible some people are going to read. We tend to copy what we see and model what we encounter daily. So, we must live a life that leaves a favorable impact on people. Like a child, adults learn from others they are around. The Bible says, "Don't let your good be evil spoken of." Watch your walk! Get in a position to hear from God. Because he will speak to you and then you will be able to speak properly to the people. This makes way for God to provide good guidance to you so that you can provide it to those that you been charged to preside over. Focus on being a leader and not a boss. A leader leads through example and doesn't dictate but takes the time to show those under them. Bosses tend to order and be demanding. And they love being referred to as..." Boss". A good leader has a heart for the people. And they are strong. They know that they are only as good as those around them. They reward others that are hard working. And they are secure enough to tell others thank you and how well they're doing. In this situation everyone wins.

Terrible leaders lack transparency. They can't be real. And their ego is a real impediment to them. They don't communicate well either. And they are very inconsistent. Bad leaders ride employees all the time. As a Christian we tend to want people to know our titles. But we need to glorify God. It doesn't benefit the body of Christ when we work to let people know you're the leader. That's a red flag. In these instances, it's a manifestation of how powerless we are beyond work. It's an extension of how miserable that person really is. So how do poor leaders rectify their shortcomings? They must own it. Leading by example is a must, because our lives are sometimes the only Bible some people will ever read. Some people will never pick a Bible up, but they will study you. We are a lot like those around us. We tend to model what we see, hear and experience. So, we can impact people by our actions as leaders. Like professional athletes, entertainers, politicians and other noteworthy individuals, everyday leaders are in the spotlight too at a different level. The scriptures say, "Train up a child in the direction in which you will have he or she to go and when the child is old, he or she will not depart from the way he or she was raised." Like children, adults sometimes reflect in our words, actions and deeds what we see those in charge doing. As a result, we must live a life resembling what the Bible recognizes as a good way of living. First, leaders must position themselves to hear from God. In fact, some leaders act as though they are God himself. God will speak to you as a leader and then you can adequately communicate to the people, if a leader humbles him or herself, puts ego aside and communicates the instructions provided by The Most High this pleases God. A lot of times we're operating in the flesh instead of the spirit. But it takes being still so that we can hear from God.

We must be guarded about what we expose ourselves to so

that we can get good directions. Good leaders are strong people. They find people that mirror themselves to ensure success. They know that it takes a team to get things done. They don't mind giving a good evaluation. They complement their workers. They don't mind rewarding those that do good for them. The online Biblical reference site Bible Study Tools says, "Being a leader takes courage, discipline, and determination. While a great leader can bring great success, it also comes at the cost of being judged and overwhelmed. The Bible speaks of so many wonderful leaders and how God blessed them for their work. There are many verses and Scriptures that God spoke to encourage men and women who choose to step up and lead. If you are striving to be a leader or if you need inspiration along the way, these Bible verses about leadership should help!" Some include Matthew 20:26 "…whoever wants to be great among you must be your servant." Matthew 7:12 "So in everything do to others as you would have them to do to you, for this sums up the law and the prophets." In 1 Timothy 3:2 it says, "The leader must be above reproach, faithful to his wife, temperate, self-controlled, respectable, hospitable, able to teach." A favorite of mine about leadership is Philippians 2: 3-4 "Do nothing out of selfish ambition or vain conceit. Rather in humility, value others above yourself. Not looking to your own interests, but to the interests of others." There are many other Biblical references concerning leadership. However, these are tried and true references that have worked for those looking to provide good reliable leadership.

God is the ultimate leader. As a result, we should be modeling ourselves after him using his word as a resource to ensure our success as leaders and a legacy that speaks favorably to our presiding over others. How we lead should shift the paradigm. Move the needle. Change the game. And if we infuse the word of God into our efforts as we work hard for those that we serve; we should be just fine. In an October 23, 2016 article written by Penn State students in an applied social psychology blog titled: *The Traits of a Good Leader: Dr. Martin Luther King Jr.*, it states, "Leadership is a process whereby an individual influence a group of individuals to achieve a common goal." This is a good reference because it provides clarity about what leadership is and how it should look. Let's work in THIS respect leaders!

You Can't Hurt People Without Hurting Yourself

Galatians 6:7-9
Be not deceived; God is not mocked for whatsoever a man soweth, that shall he also reap.

1 Peter 5:3
Not domineering over those in your charge, but being examples to the flock

We must be careful about the way we treat people, because whatever seed we put into the ground is what it will come up as later. We reap what we sow. As a result, we should treat others how we want to be treated. When we try to put stumbling blocks in others way without just cause, we are creating a distraction designed to hurt others, but in the process, we are building a wall that keeps us back as well. It's like continuing to sit in a person's lap when they want to get up. Both parties can't move forward because one is intentionally sitting and the other is busy trying to get up. In the end, neither one progresses because they're working against the will of the other. Each person in this instance is losing.

It takes so much effort to hold others back. When we try to hurt others, it's going to come back to us. And in today's world, it doesn't take long until we see it again. Setting traps, plotting and scheming is not recommended. For instance, some like to advance by way of telling on others on the job and undermining the efforts of their co-workers. But be careful! Because that might be you getting undermined next. When we work to destroy others, in the end we hurt ourselves. Doing this is like a boomerang. It's call karma. The scripture says, "Vengeance is mine, thus said The Lord". How do we respond when we are aware that others are plotting against us and we know it? We must forgive, stay focus, stay close to God and let him handle our affairs. I once worked in a salon where a co-worker didn't like a particular customer. When asked what it was about the customer that made her dislike her, our co-worker replied, "I just don't like her. She hasn't done anything to me, but I just don't like her." But her judgement was unfounded and without justification and based strictly on her personal issue with that customer just because, not because the customer had done something to deserve our co-worker's disposition.

There was once a young lady during my evangelism, that kept avoiding me each time I tried to pray for her. It was puzzling until I found out that she didn't care for me. As far as I and others could tell, it wasn't because I had done something along the way to hurt her. And while she didn't take her distain for me to an extreme level, she talked wrongly about me. Her actions did serve as a block and kept me from praying for her, which could have been a blessing to her. In this situation, she missed an additional opportunity to be covered because she chose to let her unjustified dislike for me to take precedent over me praying for her. Since then she has gone through a bit of turmoil part of which could have been brought on by her not letting me pray for her for superficial reasons coupled with speaking lies about me to others. Again, you can't her hurt others without hurting yourself. I could have helped her. So, when I see others trying to cause others hurt and pain for no reason it concerns me. Remember. No weapon formed against the righteous shall prosper. Remember. Touch not my anointed one and do my prophet no harm. Like the award-winning Hip-Hop artist **MC Hammer** said in his classic song, "Can't touch this!"

Adopt this attitude when you are being tried by those doing things to hurt you without a reason and I assure you that you will prevail because of…and in spite of…their attempts to do you harm without a reason. It was Sister Ellen Miller that caused me to adopt this position through her encouragement and assurance when sharing with her my challenges regarding people trying to hurt me without a reason. I encourage you to take her advice as well. In addition, choose to rise above your distractors efforts to harm you. Pastor **T D Jakes** says the things that hurt us the most can become the fuel and the catalyst that propel us toward our destiny. It will either make you bitter or make you better. Choose better. I have many reasons to be bitter with those that tried to hurt me intentionally throughout my life. But I instead chose to count it all joy. Choose better!

A lot of chaos can be happening all around you but like Christ, you have peace in the middle of the storm. The enemy will try to distract you. The devil comes to kill, steal and destroy. But when you have confidence and trust in God you will win. When you know who you belong to that's very valuable. If we continue to live right and do that what is pleasing to him, then we can't lose. But what about when we must just safeguard against hurt because others choose to do damage anyway? I would guard my heart. Get lost in the word of God. Get around positive people that speak good into your life. Stay busy doing positive things. If I'm causing the hurt, then I would still find the word of God. In addition, I would seek out those in this case as well that speak that which is helpful to me in getting better and improving. Someone that will say, "Hey you're doing the wrong thing. Don't take that path." Because it's important who we choose as friends. When we do this God is pleased. The closer you walk with him, the less we'll get involved in activities that are not pleasing to him. This is when we begin to grow.

Growing gracefully is a blessing. This is me. I have evolved by God's mercy, grace and my maturation. As a result, I'm no longer subject to retaliating when wronged. This makes God smile when we rise above pettiness. The battle is the Lord's. Remember. When we rush to do evil to others without justification, we can expect evil in our own house

Lead Where We Want Others to Go

Matthew 5:16
In the same way, let your light shine before others, so that they may see your good works and give glory to your father which is in heaven

1 Peter 5:3
Not domineering over those in your charge, but being examples to the flock

Leaders must be willing to go into the unknown. They are walking examples. Practicing what they say is important. Unfortunately, there are leaders whose lives belie what they are preaching. Let's stretch ourselves to go higher. Let's get outside of our boxes. Let's try new and innovative things to help build God's kingdom. But it takes courage. World renown American born evangelist **Billy Graham** described courage as contagious. He further pointed out years ago while still preaching that, "when a brave man takes a stand, the spines of others is often stiffened." It's all about building the kingdom. We have it twisted. Kingdom building is helping the people get to God through righteous conduct and behavior.

Tradition is an example of what can hinder us from growing and helping those we lead to grow. It has a lot of us in prison without bars. A lot of people are in a living hell because of tradition. We go through the motions of worshipping for instance but can't retain and make the word live because we are lost in tradition. Our first love and most powerful resource of getting the masses to follow is through teaching the word of God. While we enjoy, respect and appreciate the aspects of worship that make us feel good, i.e., the songs, dressing up and the delivery of the word, we must respectfully challenge ourselves to provide parishioners with practical ways of navigating life's pitfalls. Our followers then respect their leaders more. They feel better because they see their growth and the growth of those presiding over them. Everybody wins in this situation. But leaders must first be in the position to hear from God. It takes getting away to a place of solitude. Fasting and praying is a means by which this can be done. This positions leaders to be better examples. This helps us hear God better. It cleanses us and lets us hear him clearer.

For instance, womanizing is a hinderance to the man of God striving to hear from God and hearing him loud and clear. Because this activity is rooted in the exchange of spirits, feelings and pleasure, is can be a tremendous distraction and a deterrent regarding hearing from God and getting clear correct guidance for those that leader has been given charge over. Staying clear of this kind of activity let's one clearly hear from God and do the unusual or something different for God and his people. Because if he's in it your effort it will be blessed.

What to Do When We Don't Know

Psalm 25: 4-5
Show me the right path O Lord; point out the road for me to follow. Lead me by your truth and teach me, for you are the God that saves me. All day long I put my hope in you

Jeremiah 33:3
Call unto me, and I   will answer thee, and show thee great and mighty things, which thou knowest not

Psalms 32:8

I   will instruct thee and teach thee in the way which though shalt go I will guide **thee** *with thine eye*

When we don't know, we need to get training, assistance or help from those that do. Because we don't know everything. When we don't know, seek help! Seek wise counsel. The word tells us to seek wise counsel. In today's world, there is a plethora of resources available in addition to traditional ones. There's Google and YouTube. There's the internet. For instance, a boy can't adequately learn from a woman as well as he can from a man. On the other hand, if there's a women's conference taking place for example, it would be better planned and coordinated by a woman, since it's designed to reach and assist those who share the same needs and experiences as the planner. If a person of the cloth has trouble with putting a sermon together, then confer with people that are good at constructing the pastor's thoughts and recommendations. There's nothing wrong with admitting that we don't know. We can't let pride, ego or arrogance keep us from seeking help. The late gospel music great Reverend **James Cleveland** said, "You can't fix what you can't face." Leaders must be especially careful. Trying to proceed under these circumstances is a trick of the enemy. We can't act like we are the one if we don't know what we're doing at the time. We can't act like we're the only one that gets something done.

God gave us gifts to serve humanity. Let people work in their gifts. If we don't know how to get something done, then look for others that have that talent or expertise to ensure the success of our effort. Some leaders don't have the ability to connect with people easily. Others can't articulate their points very well. To overcome our shortcomings, we must admit that we need some help, find a way to overcome the obstacle, and then commence to letting those that can help be successful doing what they do. When you have more information as a leader and you allow people to work in their gifts, then you lead better. This is when growth will happen. Change will occur. If you have a congregation for instance and take on this attitude and intent, your numbers will increase along with your ministries and other areas. This is because the leader is doing it for all the right reasons and is prospering because he or she is capitalizing on the gifts of the spirit and those around he or she that are a gift and gifted.

At the end of the day seek God and he will show you

what's right for you. He will direct us back to the right path. God leads those that obey him with his unfailing love and faithfulness. Don't try to figure it out for yourself. Ask God for help.

Let the Work You've Done Speak for You

Matthew 6:34
Therefore, do not be anxious about tomorrow, for tomorrow will be anxious for itself, enough for the day of its own trouble.

We're going to spend an eternity somewhere following our physical time on this plain. It may be heaven; it may be hell. The way we live each day is our story…a picture of our time spent here. What should it look like? How should it be interpreted by those coming behind us? How should history treat us? When people see you coming what do they say about you? The Bible

says, "A good name is better than chosen riches". It makes me feel good when people compliment me. Because I want to be a light. The way we live our lives is important. The way we treat and talk to others will be how we will be written about and spoken of later. Therefore, we must be guarded concerning our activities. Where we go, what we do while there and how we treat people along the way will determine how we will be remembered and most of all, how God thinks of us. Secular activities are always there. Temptations are lying in wait. However, we must be in the world but not of it. Have fun. But do it in moderation and always in good taste. We must be careful. I had the opportunity to preach my uncle Reverend Walter Louis McGhee's funeral. I reminded those present that while he didn't have a lot of money or material wealth, he was a good man that cared about his family. He was about God's business.

Show love in your walk and talk. Be about your father's business.

Establishing, maintaining and leaving a good name behind you is the important legacy you can create. Our daily walk may be the only Bible some people ever read. It may be a reference for many. My niece used say, "I want to be like Auntie Debra. She's got it going on." This did my heart a world of good. That's because her impression of me was so amazing that she wanted to emulate me. I was honored and humbled by her revelation because it was confirmation that my daily walk was not in vain, but an asset to God and the world. It will help to blessed people looking on if we live a beautiful life. We will be better able to impress others. Motivate them. Alter poor behavior. And convince them to live a life like ours for the purpose of pleasing God and helping humanity to be better. The choices we make don't just affect us; they impact everyone around us. The choices we make today will affect our tomorrow.

Become Intimate with God

1 John 2:3-6
Now by this we know that we know him, if we keep his commandments He who says, "I know Him, and does not keep his commandments, is a liar and the truth is not in him but whoever keeps his word, truly the love of God is perfected in him By this we know that we are in him. He who says he abides in Him ought himself also to walk just as He walked.

Our relationship with God should be beautiful. When we become intimate with him, we benefit greatly. It might be reading the scriptures. It might be praying to him. It might be fasting. These practices allow us to walk closer to God and positions us to better hear from him, properly interpret him and manifest his desires. This allows us to become full of the Holy Spirit. The more we get this inside of us the better examples we will be. We will become better disciples. That's what we want to do. Be good examples of what

Christ lived and taught. I would be a shame to have lived all this life and to end up in a lake of fire anyway! And being good isn't enough. There must be some intimacies with God. Because if we have a lot of him in us, it will show. We are known by the fruit that we bear. Exuding pure love is essential. That comes by growing gracefully in God. It's a beautiful look and it feels good on the inside. It provides peace and comfort. I'm in a much better place as a result. It hasn't always been the case with me. There's still room for improvement in me. But when you know that you know God, that's a beautiful thing. And like that **Earth, Wind and Fire** classic said, it should show on our faces… and through our words and actions.

Rejection Is for Your Protection

1 Peter 4: 12-13
Beloved think it not strange concerning the fiery trial which is to try you as though some strange thing happened to you. But rejoice in as much as ye are partakers of Christ's sufferings; that, when his glory shall be revealed, you may be glad also with exceeding joy

Rejection is definitely for your protection! In my life I have had the wonderful opportunity to be rejected. Yes! I did say wonderful. I couldn't see it then, but I learned many things when I was rejected. I was rejected in many ways by people. This included church, family, friends, co-workers and ministerial acquaintances. When I wasn't included and even looked over by not being invited, I once thought that was the most horrible thing but what I learned was much more valuable. I learned that my rejection was God protecting me. He was saying that I was better than any occasion that I wasn't invited to.

He said I am guarding your anointing. It was all for the glory of God. He said that the same people that rejected you, you will have to go back and pick them up. I couldn't see that, but Sister

Miller reminded me to be thankful when you are not invited or included. She said, "You're one of God's greatest to him." She reminded me that the rejection was saving my life. I found out that if I had not been rejected; I would not have any testimonies. I would not have any books to write. I would not be a motivational speaker, teacher, author or entrepreneur. When we are rejected, we must not get stuck doing the rejection. We must count it all joy and move on. Thank God for the rejection.

The Wind Doesn't Blow the Same Always!

Ecclesiastes 3:1
There is a time for everything, and a season for every activity under the heavens

Hebrews 13:8
Jesus Christ is the same yesterday and today and forever

Things don't always turn out the same way. You may have gotten good results from one thing and then something very similar to that you thought that you were going to get the same results from, you didn't. If you are outside notice that when the wind blows, it blows in many different directions. It could be a soft wind or often a very harsh wind depending upon the weather. The fact is that the wind is constantly changing. Just like everyday lives are constantly changing. Our economy is changing. Our bodies are changing. Our families, incomes, status, our jobs, our personal situations are changing. Very often things don't always go the way that you plan for them to. Sometimes you might think that just because it was like that on yesterday it will be the same today. However, there will be changes in the church, ministry, leaders and other places that will not be the same on today. We must be able to deal with the change and keep moving forward.

For example: It's like baking a cake. Sometimes when baking a cake, it never turns out the same every time even though there are the same ingredients. It has the same temperature and it still does not turn out the same way every time. We can't say if change happens in our lives what will we have to do. When changes come into our lives, we must be able to deal with the change whether it's good or bad. But in life you must find a way to work through the changes. You must pray for wisdom and patience and guidance. God will see you through it. We must know what the scriptures say in Romans 8: 28 "And we know that all things work together for good to those who love the Lord to those who are called according to his purpose." He didn't say that all things are going to be good always, but it will work together for good. There are times when we don't know what to do but we need to seek God for the changes and listen to him. Meanwhile we must thank God for the change whether good or bad. While thinking we must think on things that are positive and pleasing to him. Whenever you go through your change, go through it with the right attitude. Remember the old saying, your attitude determines your altitude; Your altitude determines how high you go. Be ready for the change because change is evitable. Meanwhile praise him during the process.

What You Feed Will Grow, What You Starve Will Die

1 Peter 5:8
Be sober minded; be watchful; your *adversity the devil prowls around like a roaring lion seeking someone to devour.*

Philippians 4:8
Finally, brothers and sisters, whatever is true, whatever is noble, whatever is right, whatever is pure, whatever is lovely, whatever is admirable-if anything is excellent or praiseworthy think about such things

Whatever you feed will grow. If you give a plant some fertilizer, sunlight and water, then it will grow. Same thing applies to our lives. If you have a baby, we all know that the baby needs to be fed. As you feed the baby, then the baby begins to grow too. It's a newborn, a year old, two, three and before you know it, the child's grown. Well the baby had to be fed and nourished. The same thing happens when life rolls you out situations that may not be good for you or even negative. It will influence you. If you feed into unpleasant situations or conversations, then the condition will begin to grow. It will grow and grow if you continue to talk about them over and over. Mother Ellen told me that it will get in your spirit because it is growing simply because you fed it. Stop rehearsing situations repeatedly. Let it go! Give it to God. I did. I'm reminded of it!

There was some negativity going on about me personally. It was the most terrible mistruth one could ever create. I immediately knew that it wasn't true. I myself personally have learned not to chase lies but this one touched me just for a moment, but I immediately thought about how Jesus was accused repeatedly. His name was scandalized. He suffered. He died for our sins and I realize that if Jesus suffered and was accused then I knew that we will be falsely accused. At first, I thought Lord why? But then I thought to myself why not? I learned from this situation that when we are doing a mighty work for the Lord, the enemy is mad. He doesn't want you manifest what God has given you. I said Father, forgive them Lord for they do not know what they do. (Luke 23:34). Isaiah

54:17 says, "No weapon formed against you shall prosper and every tongue that rises up against you shall be condemned."

I learned from that situation and many others that negativity will come. I have too much that God has chosen me to do for him. It was a trick of the enemy in order to get me off course from the calling that God has on my life. It was nothing but a distraction. You must call it out for what it really is. I began to fast and pray and talk to Mother Miller about this and she encouraged me to not feed this. This is truly a distraction. Let it die! God says he is going to fix it all.

I received that word and confirmation that God was going to handle it and then I began to laugh at the Devil. I just laughed. I thought about how God had fixed every situation in my life before. I thought about the anointing that God had placed on my life. I thought even about the scripture that says in Psalms 105: 15 "Touch Not my anointed ones and do my prophet no harm." I said I'm not just Debra. I am an anointed woman of God and people can't do me any kind of way. God always has fought every battle for me in the past and then he reminded me in the form of a question. Why are you trying to fight a battle that is already won? I continue to this day to rejoice in this. Turning all my situations over to God. I simply let Go and let God fight my battles for me. I am a witness. He will do it. He said in Deuteronomy "Vengeance is mine. I will repay you." Have you ever had a situation happen in your life, and you fed it? Well from now on don't feed into things that are not important. Give it to God.

Don't feed into it! Let it Go! Let Go and Let God. He's got it!

Your Giving Says A Lot About You

Luke 6:38

Give and it shall be given unto; Good Measure, pressed down, shaken together and running *over shall men give unto your* bosom

God wants us to give our Time, Our tithe and our Talents. For the scripture says Bring all the tithes into the storehouse. If you notice, people that give abundantly and cheerfully reap abundance. If you sew sparingly, you will reap sparingly. God loves a cheerful giver. You need to give because it's the right thing to do. Sister Miller always encourages me to Love,

Live and Give. John 3:16 in the Bible says, "For God so loved the world that he gave his only begotten son that whosoever believe in him shall not perish but shall have everlasting life." He gave his only son. That's love. He gave without any regrets. That's love. No remorse. He gave freely. There was no greater love than for him to lay down his life for his friend, us. He was our friend when we were his enemy. We helped put him on the cross because we did not know him. The bible says except he draws then we can't come to him. God does the drawing. He gave something to us so we could have something to give to him. He said give and it shall be given unto you; pressed down shaken together; running over shall men give unto his bosom.

We must give our Time, Tithe and Talent. We must give our tithes and offering freely. When we give, we must do it as though we are giving unto the Lord. We cannot worry about what happens to it after we have given because we did the right thing according to the word. Living our lives as Jesus lived is a beautiful thing. Yes, there will be bumps in the road, but we can do our part to learn of Jesus's ways. We can live a better life by reading his word, adopting his character, attending bible study, gathering with other believers and applying biblical principles to our lives. We should live our lives following Christ. We should live like Jesus lived. Jesus Loved, Jesus Lived, He gave, and he forgives.

You Are as Good as Anyone

Psalms 139:14
I praise you because I am fearfully and wonderfully made;
your works are **wonderful***, I know that full well.*

Ruth Hartley Mosley said, "Never let the fact that you don't have anything keep you from achieving." These words of this Savannah born, and Macon bred Black legend of the 1930's-1970's are to be remembered. While she came from humble beginnings, she achieved great things. This quote lets all of us know that we are just as good as anyone. Mrs. Mosley was the first black registered nurse in Middle Georgia. She was a business owner. She was a globetrotter that traveled abroad. She was a socialite that owned a mansion near downtown Macon. She was a facilitator of activities during the Civil Rights movement in Macon. She was a Pioneer for women. She had many struggles in her life and came from nothing however she didn't let that stop her. Overtime, she became very well off and successful.

You may have come from nothing. You may have grown up without anything. This is not about where we have been. It's about where we are going. It doesn't matter. You are as good as anyone. You are as good as the millionaires, billionaires, wealthy and talented. You are somebody. When God has something for you to do you must do it. It doesn't matter if you don't have anything. If you have dreams, goals, visions, and a mind then you can achieve anything that you want to if you only believe. There were many times in my life that I felt unworthy, undeserving, and unappreciated. But I kept on and often was reminded if God was for me, who could be against me?

I had to keep in my life trusting God while knowing that I could do all things in life through Christ that strengthens me. Through the difficult times in my life and the unfairness of the world I had to turn my whole life over to God and began writing the vision. God delivered me and now I owe him my life. If you can believe it, you certainly can achieve it. If you put your mind to it, you can do it.

Whatever your goals are strive toward them. Know that you are special to God. He Loves us the same. I admonish you to look into the mirror and know that you are somebody to God. You are his child and you have purpose in your life. Always remember that you are truly fearfully and wonderfully made.

In Closing

Psalm 118:22
The stone which the builders rejected has become the chief cornerstone.

I hope this book was a blessing to you. I pray that at least one group of these words of wisdom speak into your life and spirit. My desire is for what you read to be a source of motivation, inspiration and hope concerning righteous living. These words of wisdom have really impacted my life and therefore I wanted to share them with you. God has blessed me to be connected to Mother Ellen Miller and what she has in her life. She has helped me to be the woman of God that I am today.

In closing I have included additional quotes from famous people that resonate loudly because of the content of the quotes and the power they possess when adhered to. I admonish you to keep them and these words of wisdom within these pages close to you and apply them to your life. I guarantee that if you do, you will be blessed and prosper in everything that you do. Blessings! ~ **Dr. Debra McGhee Shipp**

It's a blessing and privilege to be recognized as a source of strength and as a guide to my spiritual daughter Debra Shipp. I'm so proud of her for her courage and commitment to the kingdom and people of God. What she placed in these pages is what God gave me for her and you throughout my life. I too hope that it proves a blessing to you as you aspire to becoming more Christ like. More loving. More kind. This is our obligation to each other and I'm so pleased that Debra left this legacy of good as a testament to the greatness of God, and as a dedication to me as her spiritual guide and friend for life.

Today, good guidance is necessary to ensure that we're working in accordance to what is pleasing to God. This book is a part of kingdom building. Your investment in it, is an example of that. Thank you for supporting Debra. May God be pleased with this work. And may he continue to provide us with the peace that surpasses all human understanding.

~ **Sister Mother Ellen Miller**

Words of Wisdom

"Every Great dream begins with a dreamer. You have within you the strength, the patience and the passion to reach for the stars to change the world." —Harriet Tubman, Abolitionist and Leader of the Underground Railroad

Be a visionary. And bold enough to manifest what you've been given as a gift. -D.S.

"The time is always right to do what is right."
—Dr. Martin Luther King, Jr., Civil Rights icon and Drum Major for Justice for all

No matter what your situation is…. Only do what is right. Not what is popular but what is right. -D.S.

"Have a vision. Be demanding."
—Colin Powell, First Black Joint Chief of Staff of the United States

Without a vision …. The people parish. Write the vision. Make it plain. -D.S.

"Success is to be measured not so much by the position that one has reached in life as by the obstacles which he has overcome while trying to succeed."
—Booker T. Washington, founder of Tuskegee Institute, Black activist and educator

Have faith and trust yourself. Be persistent believing that you will succeed. -D.S.

"Hold fast to dreams, for if dreams die, life is a broken winged bird that cannot fly."
—Langston Hughes, award winning writer and famous Harlem Renaissance figure

Never give up on your dreams! If God gave them to you, reach for the stars. Don't let go of them. -D.S.

"If there is no struggle, there is no progress."
—Frederick Douglass, Abolitionist, statesman and orator

It makes us like the butterfly from a cocoon. Struggle makes us stronger. -D.S.

"Your true character is most accurately measured by how you treat those who can do 'nothing' for you.
— Mother Teresa, world famous nun and humanitarian

Do for others just because sometimes. Not for something in return. -D.S.

"The biggest challenge we all face is to learn about ourselves and understand our strengths and weaknesses..." —Dr.   Mae Jemison, engineer, physician and NASA's first   Black female astronaut

Learn yourself, acknowledge what needs improving and become better. -D.S.

"Bringing the gifts my ancestors gave, I am the dream and the hope of the slave. I rise. I rise. I rise."
—Maya Angelou, U.S. Poet Laurette, actress, human rights advocate

Rise. It can be done with determination and God's help. Rise! -D.S.
"We all require and want respect, man or woman, black or white. It's our basic human right." —Aretha Franklin, Grammy award winning singer and humanitarian

Simply…Respect Yourself and Learn to respect others. -D.S.

"You've got to learn to leave the table when love's no longer being served." —Nina Simone, internationally renowned singer and entertainment activist

You matter too. When you're no longer appreciated and respected move on. -D.S.

"We did not come to fear the future. We came here to shape it."
—Barack Hussein Obama, First Black President of the United States

We are the ones we've been hoping and praying for. Let's change things. -D.S.

"We need more light about each other. Light creates understanding, understanding creates love, love creates patience, and patience creates unity." —Malcolm X, Freedom fighter, activist and minister

Like the oneness of God, let's work towards the unification of hearts, minds and souls – D.S.

QUOTES AND RESEARCH REFERENCES

1. Wikipedia

2. A-Z Quotes

3. King James Version of The Holy Bible

4. Google

5. Bible Tools

6. Penn State University Student Blog

Dr. **Debra McGhee Shipp** is a native of Fort Valley, Georgia and daughter of the late S.B. and Joann McGhee. She attended Peach County High School in her hometown and holds numerous advanced degrees.

They included Bachelor of Arts and Master of Science degrees in Early Childhood Education from Fort Valley State University; an Educational Specialist degree in Elementary Education from Troy State University in Phoenix City, Alabama; and a Doctorate degree in Instructional Leadership from the University of Argosy in Sarasota, Florida.

Dr. Shipp is the Founder and Leader of the *Chat and Chew Ministry* of Macon and Middle Georgia, a communications platform designed to spiritually empower Christians internally and externally through the discussion of common life issues.

Dr. Shipp gives God all the credit for her success. She is a concerned citizen and community volunteer with a variety of awards, an accomplished educator, motivational speaker, life coach and entrepreneur.

She is married to Dr. John Todd Shipp with whom she shares her life. Dr. Shipp and her husband reside in Macon, Georgia.

To Contact Dr. Shipp email her at debrashipp1@gmail.com.

NOTES

This section is dedicated to note taking.

Notes

Notes

Notes

Notes

Notes

Notes

Notes

Notes

Notes

Notes

THANKS FOR CHOOSING ADVICE FOR LIFE BOOK

I HOPE YOU FIND INSPIRATION AND GROWTH SKILLS.

Stay Tuned for more great works on advice for life.